New Frontiers of Space

Cutting-Edge

Black Holes
Research

Kevin Kurtz

Lerner Publications ◆ Minneapolis

Copyright © 2020 by Lerner Publishing Group, Inc.

Lerner Publications Company
An imprint of Lerner Publishing Group, Inc.
241 First Avenue North
Minneapolis, MN 55401 USA

For reading levels and more information, look up this title at www.lernerbooks.com.

Main body text set in Adrianna Regular.
Typeface provided by Chank.

Library of Congress Cataloging-in-Publication Data

The Cataloging-in-Publication Data for *Cutting-Edge Black Holes Research* is on file at the Library of Congress.
ISBN 978-1-5415-5582-2 (lib. bdg.)
ISBN 978-1-5415-7483-0 (pbk.)
ISBN 978-1-5415-5672-0 (eb pdf)

Manufactured in the United States of America
1-46037-43360-4/9/2019

Contents

Chapter 1

INTO A BLACK HOLE

Deep in the Milky Way galaxy, a star is being destroyed. The gases that make up the star are being ripped from its surface. The stream of gases swirls around, like water going down a drain. Then it vanishes.

A black hole rips gas from the surface of a star.

A black hole is destroying the star. A black hole is an object with so much gravity that nothing can escape from it—not even light. Because black holes trap light, we can't see them with optical telescopes. But astronomers use other tools to observe black holes. They can even see black holes "eating" stars. As astronomers study black holes, they are learning amazing things.

Black holes are invisible, so even the biggest optical telescopes can't see them.

A Look Inside

Black holes are the most massive objects in the universe. A massive object has a lot of stuff in it. The more massive an object is, the more it weighs. Massive doesn't always mean big though. Many black holes are small. If Earth became a black hole, all the material that makes up our planet would be packed into a space smaller than a marble. But it would still weigh just as much.

Gases and other material swirl around a supermassive black hole at the center of a distant galaxy.

Astronomers think that black holes have two parts. The event horizon is the outer edge of a black hole. Nothing inside the event horizon can escape the black hole. Even light cannot escape.

The second part of a black hole is the singularity. In the singularity, all the matter in the black hole is packed into a tiny point. It is smaller than an atom. A singularity contains so much stuff that it does not follow the normal rules of the universe. Scientists think that time and space do not exist there.

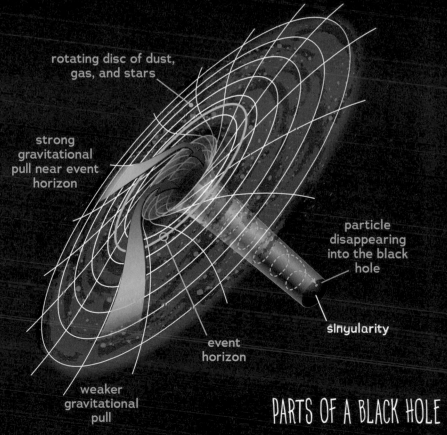

rotating disc of dust, gas, and stars

strong gravitational pull near event horizon

particle disappearing into the black hole

singularity

event horizon

weaker gravitational pull

PARTS OF A BLACK HOLE

Meet the Black Hole Family

Astronomers have discovered different kinds of black holes. Stellar black holes form when giant stars run out of fuel. The stars are crushed by their own gravity. Most stellar black holes are five to ten times as massive as our sun. But even with all this matter, they may be only as wide as a small city on Earth. Astronomers have found stellar black holes in our galaxy, the Milky Way.

To measure the mass of a black hole, astronomers compare it to the mass of our sun.

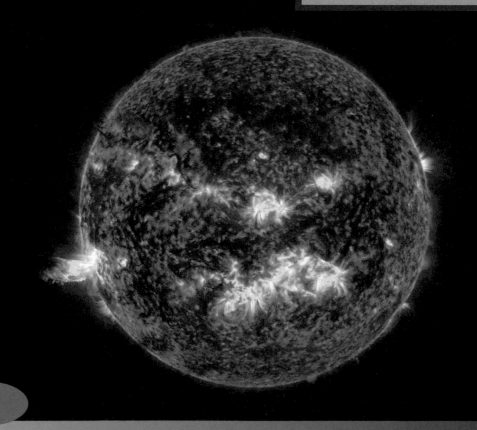

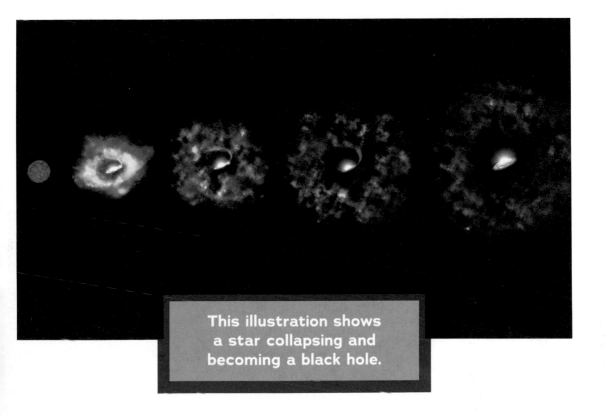

This illustration shows a star collapsing and becoming a black hole.

Sometimes two stellar black holes crash into each other. They merge and become a larger black hole. Astronomers call this an intermediate black hole. Astronomers have not found many intermediate black holes.

Supermassive black holes are millions to billions of times more massive than our sun. The smallest ones are about twenty times as wide as our sun. The biggest ones are larger than our whole solar system. They get bigger as they "eat" stars and other space objects.

Astronomers are not sure how supermassive black holes form. One idea is that many smaller black holes merge, over billions of years, to form supermassive black holes.

Two black holes orbit each other. They might merge to become an even bigger black hole.

TIMELINE OF THE UNIVERSE FOLLOWING THE BIG BANG

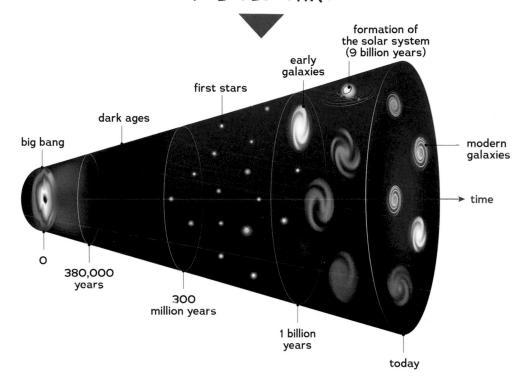

big bang

dark ages

first stars

early galaxies

formation of the solar system (9 billion years)

modern galaxies

time

0

380,000 years

300 million years

1 billion years

today

The big bang created our universe. During this event, a singularity containing all the matter in existence suddenly exploded. The matter became stars, planets, gases, and other objects.

The big bang might have produced small black holes called primordial black holes. Astronomers think they are less massive than our sun. Astronomers have never found one though.

Space Fact or Fiction?

Particle colliders could create a tiny black hole that could destroy Earth.

This is fiction. Particle colliders send subatomic particles, or particles smaller than atoms, smashing into one another. The Relativistic Heavy Ion Collider, in New York, started up in 2000. The Large Hadron Collider, in Switzerland and France, began operating in 2008. Some people worried that particle collisions there would create tiny black holes. But particle colliders don't create black holes. These machines just allow scientists to observe particle collisions. That helps scientists learn more about the tiny particles that make up atoms, living things, and everything else in the universe.

Chapter 2

"SEEING" BLACK HOLES

Since black holes are invisible, astronomers have devised other ways to find and watch them. One way is to look for objects that seem to be orbiting empty space. They might be stars or clouds of gas and dust caught by a black hole's gravity.

In this illustration, large amounts of gas swirl around a supermassive black hole.

Radio telescopes such as these can detect radio waves from black holes.

As these objects drain into the black hole, they spin at incredible speeds. The swirling objects also heat up. They release tremendous amounts of energy, such as radio waves. The waves travel through space. Astronomers can use radio telescopes to detect them.

"Listening" to Black Holes

Scientists also detect black holes by searching for gravitational waves. Movement creates gravitational waves. They spread out through space like waves traveling across water. Gravitational waves are similar to sound waves. Scientists can even turn them into sound and listen to things happening far away in the universe.

This illustration shows gravitational waves spreading out from the collision of two black holes.

More than one billion years ago, two stellar black holes smashed into each other. One black hole was thirty-six times as massive as the sun. The other was twenty-nine times as massive as the sun. The collision was one of the most violent events since the big bang. It sent gravitational waves through the universe.

This computer-generated image shows two black holes colliding.

LIGO uses giant ground-based antennae to detect gravitational waves from black holes.

The collision took place trillions of miles away from Earth. It took 1.3 billion years for the gravitational waves from the collision to reach our planet. The Laser Interferometer Gravitational-Wave Observatory (LIGO) detected the waves in 2015. This was the first time astronomers ever detected gravitational waves.

Inside LIGO

LIGO opened in 2015. The observatory has two stations. One is in Washington State, and one is in Louisiana. The stations use giant L-shaped antennae to detect gravitational waves. Each antenna is 2.5 miles (4 km) long and runs along the ground. LIGO can detect tiny gravitational waves—thousands of times smaller than an atom.

GRAVITATIONAL WAVES FROM THE COLLISION OF TWO BLACK HOLES TRAVEL THROUGH TRILLIONS OF MILES OF SPACE.

▼

LIGO has detected gravitational waves from several black hole collisions. It can turn gravitational waves into sounds, much as a radio converts radio waves into sounds. The sounds of a black hole collision are a little like dripping water or chirping birds.

Besides detecting gravitational waves from colliding black holes, LIGO can detect gravitational waves from supernovae. These are exploding stars. They also create gravitational waves that travel far through space.

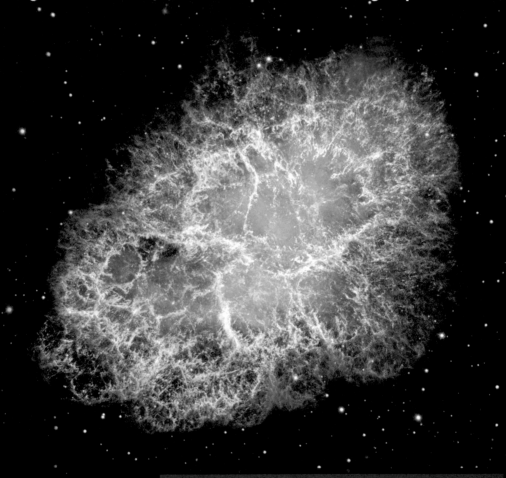

The Hubble Space Telescope captured this picture of a supernova, or exploding star.

Chapter 3

MONSTER OF THE MILKY WAY

In 1974, using radio telescopes, astronomers detected great amounts of energy coming from the center of the Milky Way. These energy bursts were a sign that something massive was there. But astronomers couldn't see it.

Since the 1970s, astronomers have searched for a supermassive black hole at the center of the Milky Way.

Using telescopes that detect infrared radiation, astronomers tracked twenty-eight stars orbiting the unknown object. By studying the orbits, astronomers figured out that the object was more than four million times more massive than our sun. Something that massive had to be a black hole.

Infrared telescopes, such as this one in Hawaii, can monitor energy from black holes and other space objects.

An artist's rendering of Sagittarius A*, the black hole at the center of the Milky Way.

In 2018, astronomers measured energy coming from gas and dust close to the black hole. They used these measurements to estimate its width. Although it is four million times more massive than the sun, it is only about eighteen times as wide. That proves that it is very dense. No doubt about it—it is a supermassive black hole.

Sagittarius A* is the supermassive black hole at the center of the Milky Way. Everything in the galaxy orbits around it. Astronomers have found supermassive black holes at the center of other galaxies too. They think that all galaxies might have supermassive black holes at their centers.

Like the Milky Way, the Andromeda galaxy probably has a supermassive black hole at its center.

A Trip to a Black Hole

The Milky Way's black holes are too far away to hurt us. But what would it be like to travel into one? If you were heading feetfirst into a stellar black hole, your feet would feel much more gravity than your head. The difference in force would be so great that it would rip your body in two. Then the two pieces of your body would get ripped apart again. This would keep happening until you were just a stream of atoms. The black hole would then slurp up the stream of atoms like a spaghetti noodle.

Chapter 4

INTO THE FUTURE

In April 2017, radio telescopes in different places on Earth pointed at Sagittarius A* and the supermassive black hole at the center of the Messier 87 galaxy. They all collected radio waves from these supermassive black holes at the same time. Astronomers used the data to create pictures of the black hole's event horizons. The project, called the Event Horizon Telescope, has allowed us to see the edges of a black hole for the very first time.

This image of Messier 87's supermassive black hole is the first picture ever taken of a black hole's event horizon.

THE CHANDRA X-RAY OBSERVATORY DETECTS X-RAY BURSTS FROM BLACK HOLES AND OTHER SPACE OBJECTS.

Space telescopes will give us more information about black holes. The Chandra X-ray Observatory is a telescope in space. As it orbits Earth, it detects X-ray bursts coming from matter swirling into black holes. The James Webb Space Telescope will go into orbit in 2021. This optical telescope will look for evidence of primordial black holes.

A Lot More to Learn

Scientists have many theories about black holes. For instance, astronomers think that black holes might

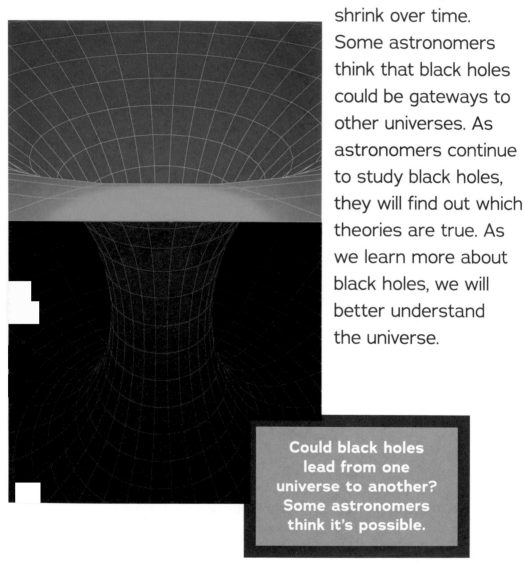

shrink over time. Some astronomers think that black holes could be gateways to other universes. As astronomers continue to study black holes, they will find out which theories are true. As we learn more about black holes, we will better understand the universe.

Could black holes lead from one universe to another? Some astronomers think it's possible.

3D Printer Activity

Do you want to see the Chandra X-ray Observatory up close? You can make a 3D-printed version of this space telescope that's searching for black holes. Visit the link below for instructions.

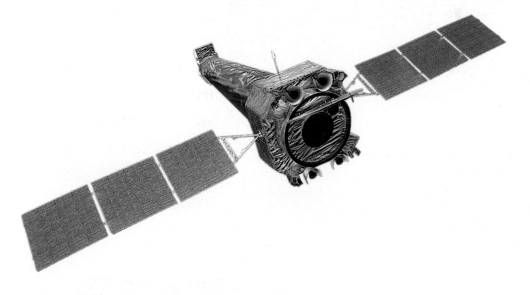

PAGE PLUS

http://qrs.lernerbooks,com/duzx

Glossary

astronomer: a scientist who studies objects and matter in space

atom: one of the most basic units of matter. An atom is more than a million times smaller than the thickness of a human hair.

event horizon: the outer boundary of a black hole. Inside the event horizon, nothing can escape the gravity of the black hole.

galaxy: a vast system of stars, planets, dust, gases, and other matter in space, all held together by gravity. Earth is part of the Milky Way galaxy.

gravity: an invisible force that attracts two bodies to each other in space or on Earth. The more massive an object is, the stronger its gravity is.

infrared radiation: invisible energy given off by warm objects

matter: what all objects are made of

orbit: to travel around something in circles. The path of an object as it circles another object in space is also an orbit.

singularity: the single point at the center of a black hole where all its matter is packed together

telescope: an instrument for detecting and observing faraway objects. Optical telescopes gather visible light to let users see distant objects. Radio telescopes collect radio waves coming from space. Other kinds of telescopes collect X-rays, infrared radiation, and other types of energy.

Learn More about Black Holes

Books

Kerrod, Robin. *Universe*. New York: DK, 2015. Read more about black holes as well as the stars, galaxies, and other objects in space that surround them.

Mara, Will. *Breakthroughs in Deep Space Science*. Minneapolis: Lerner Publications, 2019. Learn about new space discoveries and the tools that make them possible. Take a tour of black holes, exoplanets, and other wonders of space.

Roland, James. *Black Hole: A Space Discovery Guide*. Minneapolis: Lerner Publications, 2017. Read about the incredible and mind-boggling science of black holes.

Websites

Black Holes
https://kids.nationalgeographic.com/explore/space/black-holes
/#black-hole-1.jpg
National Geographic Kids describes black holes, with links to many other articles about space and space exploration.

NASA Space Place
https://spaceplace.nasa.gov
Learn about black holes, gravitational waves, and the rest of our universe.

What Do Black Holes Sound Like?
https://www.theatlantic.com/video/index/484130/what-do-black
-holes-sound-like/
Click on this animated video to learn about black holes and to hear the sounds of black holes colliding.

Index

Photo Acknowledgments

Image credits: NASA, ESA, Martin Kornmesser (ESA/Hubble), p. 4; ESO/Gianluca Lombardi, p. 5;
ESO/M. Kornmesser, p. 6; Laura Westlund/Independent Picture Service, p. 7; NASA/SDO, p. 8;
NASA, ESA, and P. Jeffries (STScI), p. 9; Science Photo Library/Alamy Stock Photo, p. 10; ttsz/
iStock/Getty Images, p. 11; Harold Cunningham/Getty Images, p. 12; NASA, ESA, the Hubble
Heritage Team (STScI/AURA), and R. Gendler (for the Hubble Heritage Team) acknowledgment,
J. GaBany, p. 13; MyLoupe/Universal Images Group/Getty Images, p. 14; MARK GARLICK/SCIENCE
PHOTO LIBRARY/Getty Images, p. 15; The Simulating eXtreme Spacetimes (SXS) Project/Science
Source, p. 16; Caltech/MIT/LIGO Lab, p. 17; Amber Stuver/Wikimedia Commons (CC BY-SA 4.0),
p. 18; ESA (CC BY-SA 3.0 IGO), p. 19; creativemarc/Shutterstock.com, p. 20; Suchart Kuathan/
Moment/Getty Images, p. 21; Roger Ressmeyer/Corbis/VCG/Getty Images, p. 22; keanu2/iStock/
Getty Images, p. 23; Robert Gendler/Stocktrek Images/Getty Images, p. 24; Mark Garlick/Science
Source, p. 25; Event Horizon Telescope Collaboration (CC BY 3.0), p. 26; NASA, p. 27; KTSDESIGN/
SCIENCE PHOTO LIBRARY/Getty Images, p. 28; NASA/CXC/SAO, p. 29.

Cover: ESO/M. Kornmesser (CC BY 4.0).